I want to be a Baker

JANICE NIBBS

THE CHOIR PRESS

Copyright © 2025 Janice Nibbs

All rights reserved. No part of this publication may be reproduced or transmitted in any form or by any means, electronic or mechanical including photocopying, recording or any information storage or retrieval system, without prior permission in writing from the publishers.

The right of Janice Nibbs to be identified as the author of this work has been asserted by her in accordance with the Copyright, Designs and Patents Act 1988

First published in the United Kingdom in 2025 by

The Choir Press

ISBN 978-1-78963-464-8 Hardback

ISBN 978-1-78963-463-1 Paperback

ISBN 978-1-78963-465-5 eBook

Illustrated by Reuben Vanterpool

This is the second book in the traditional career series that highlights and guides future generations of Virgin Islanders through life in the Virgin Islands in the early 1900s. Each book is a stand-alone volume that can be read by itself, or you can decide to collect them all. The first book in the series, *I want to be a Thatcher man*, was released in 2022.

Introduction

Life has changed for the Virgin Islander; now everyone has a stove with an oven, you can also buy baked goods from a professional bakery, or the supermarket, but in times past bread and other goods were baked regularly in a pot, on a coal pot, or over a fire built between three rocks. When this method was used the fire would be lit using coal or wood. A piece of Zink referred to as tinning was prepared by placing live coals removed from the fire on it. The pot was placed on the coal pot or the rocks, very little fire was left in this fire pit. Whatever the person needed to bake – pot breads, tarts, puddings, or cakes were placed in the pot. A pot bread was a daily occurrence, other items were made if the homemaker was inclined to have something sweet to eat. There was also a box oven. This was made from wood and lined with tinning. This was a more sophisticated oven than the pot, it was heated by placing it over an open fire pit. The most sophisticated oven of all was the brick oven made from bricks and white lime. Not everyone could afford to build a brick oven which was the property of the village baker who baked on a daily basis as a trade. Other villagers would ask and be allowed to use the brick oven to bake for special occasions. Sometimes if a family had more than one baker, they would share the oven by baking on alternate days. Their products never tasted the same so there was no competing for customers. Bread was a staple of every household and when there was nothing else to eat a child could be given a piece of bread to fill a hungry belly. This meal was often washed down with a can of Sugar and water better known as Sugg-in-water. Sugg in water was often flavored with lime; hence the name lime-Sugg in Water.

No breakfast was complete without bread and tea (water tea – hot water and sugar or bush tea – tea flavored with an herb), the most popular herbs were lemon grass, sweet barley and lime bush, milk tea – tea with milk added and cocoa tea. Coffee was drunk only by adults as it was alleged it would make children's heads hard and unable to learn.

At lunch time most children were given a piece of bread for lunch. In the evening everyone ate their main meal for the day. If there was nothing else to eat everyone ate bread.

Bread came in many flavors – pot bread or power bread when made with freshly churned butter was a bread you did not want to miss. There was coconut bread, cornmeal bread, guinea-corn bread and cassava bread, but the highest form of bread was Leven/yeast bread. Leven bread was the accepted bread eaten on Sundays and special occasions. This bread was also found in shops. Persons wishing to bought a bread with box cheese or sausage to have as a meal.

The village bakers were often women who had a shop or other outlet for their bread. They had a brick oven and baked bread every day. There were also a few men who baked; but pound cakes (a cake made with a pound of all ingredients. Flour, Sugar, Butter and 6 eggs) was their favoured item. On weekends the entire village would be filled with the smell of baking goods. Each person had their specialty Boyja, tarts, potato pudding.

Whatever was being baked mouthwatering smells would travel on the breeze letting the villagers know that someone was baking and what they had made.

After the baking was done children and sometimes adults went through the village selling baked goods. The villagers were anxiously waiting to get their share of what they had smelled . . .

Marie wanted to be a baker. Every night, her dreams were filled with the feel of dough under the heel of her hands as she kneaded it in preparation for her special bread creations. She could actually see her plat breads, her long breads, and her rolls. Her hope chest contained the items she would need when she became a baker. She had found a nice sea feather and a sea fan along the sea shore. She had asked Mr. Cook the sea captain to save her a biscuit pan and a kerocean pan. These she had cut and turned the edges to make tinning on which to bake her breads. She had some 5lb butter cans cut to make cake pans. She was waiting for extra biscuit and kerocean pans. These she would cut to make pudding pans. She would need some enamel plates in which to bake her tarts. As soon as she could find a space she would plant a banana tree so she could have banana leaves. She would use these to line her tinning when she started baking. She loved the smell when breads were being baked on Banana leaves. Every morning she awoke hoping that today was the day she got the courage to ask her mother about becoming a baker.

Today, is the day, she decides, no more putting it off. As she assists her mother with the washing, she smells the items being baked by the village bakers, and she longs for the day when she will have her own oven.

'Hmmm that smells good, she says and sniffs the air as the smell of the freshly baked breads come wafting to her on the breeze. Her mouth waters and her stomach growls, but she will need to finish her chores first before her friend Doris comes with a piece of bread for her. How she wishes her mother was a baker instead of a seamstress. Then she could learn how to bake instead of sew. Her friend Doris wanted to be a seamstress, but not Marie – she always wanted to be a baker. She would ask her mother if she and Doris could change places and they could each learn from each other's mother. Doris's mother was a very good baker with a lot of customers and her mother was also a very good seamstress; so, it would be a fair exchange. Marie says 'today I will ask mother if I could become a baker, and tell her my idea about letting Doris study to be a seamstress.'

That afternoon as she helped her mother make a pot bread Marie asked 'Mother can I go by Miss Wilda to learn to become a baker. I just love the feel of kneading dough and the smells that come from the oven as breads, boyjas, cakes, tarts and puddings are baking. I would love to be the person to put them in and take them out of the oven.'

'I wondered what you wanted to do.' Replied her mother, 'I noticed that although you helped me with hemming and sewing on buttons you never showed any interest in learning to sew anything else. Your body has started to mature and it is time for me to remove you from school and get you a skill. Soon you will be thinking of getting married and you will need a way to make your own money. You can't always depend on your husband for everything you need. You always need to have a little something put away for when you need it. I will ask Miss Wilda, I think her daughter has been asking if she can become a seamstress so I will not be left without anyone to help me.'

Marie is so excited she can hardly wait to get started.

Figure 1 Baking Bread in a pot

Figure 2 Sea Fan used for sifting flour etc.

'I already have a sea fan that I can use for a sifter' she says, looking thoughtful and a sea feather to use as a whisk.

Figure 3 Sea feather

'I will look for a bottle to use as a rolling pin and a Calabash that I can mix things in until I can buy a dish pan'.

Figure 4 Calabash can be used as a large bowl.

'I will give you two flour bags as well.' says mother.

Soon the day came for Marie to go by Miss Wilda for her first baking lesson. She took all her things tied up in a flour bag.

'I see you have bought a number of items for you to use.' said Miss Wilda when Marie arrived on her first day. 'You will not need those yet, you can leave them at home until I tell you to bring them. Today you will watch me and help with simple tasks such as greasing the baking pans, and getting all the items ready. I know you know how to beat eggs and wash butter so you can help with those tasks as well. When you come next time, I will teach you how to set yeast and mix it into the other items to make bread.'

At the end of her first day Marie arrived home tired but happy, she had watched as Miss Wilda kneaded 10lbs. of Flour.

Figure 5 Kneading flour

From this she had made titi breads, plat breads and long breads to satisfy her different customers, she allowed Marie to have a piece of dough. She watched as Marie tried to make breads that resembled hers. She taught her how to roll the ends of the rolls to make cones.

Figure 6 Tete Bread

She taught her to roll three strips of dough, line them up next to each other and plat them to make plat breads.

13

Figure 7 Long Bread

Long bread

Miss Wilda taught her to knead the dough into long cylinders to make long breads. Marie tried making each item shown from her dough. These were hers, she could take them home; she would not be able to make breads for Miss Wilda's Customers as they did not know her and would not eat anything from her. It would take many months before she would be allowed to do the complete process and customers would eat what she made, but she was allowed to take home what she made to show her mother and share with her family.

Potato pudding

On her next visit Marie helped Miss Wilda prepare potato pudding.

Figure 8 Grating items for pudding and other goodies

She grated potatoes, pumpkin, tannia and green banana together, 'not a lot of tannia and green bananas' said Miss Wilda, 'as their texture is slimy and this will show in your pudding. It will also make your pudding spoil faster. The choice will be yours weather you add them to yours when you become a baker.' She grated coconut for making the coconut milk separately. Then she watched as Miss Wilda mixed the pudding. She added the coconut milk to the grated items. 'You will need to add enough coconut milk to cook the ingredients but not too much so that it will be soggy when cooked.' explained Miss Wilda. 'You will also need to add a small amount of flour to hold the pudding together. You add sugar to sweeten it, and a dash of salt. Taste your mixture, as you want to know what it will taste like when done. The combination of salt and sugar will make for a better tasting pudding. Pudding is a hot, peppery item so we will add black pepper. Some people don't like pepper but some others can't get enough. It is your choice if you will make two mixtures or stick to one. Whatever you choose your customers will let you know how they feel. When baking pudding always leave them until last. When you are finished baking heat the oven one last time. Place your pudding in the oven and close the door. When you come next day the puddings will be ready. Baking pudding is never a one day job it takes a long time to bake a pudding.'

On each visit Marie learns something new.

Figure 9 Delicious baked goods

She learns how to make baking powder breads, Coconut breads, cornmeal breads and Ginicorn bread.

She also learns to make cakes – Pound cakes and Marble cakes.

Figure 10 Tarts

Tarts

Marie learns to make tarts – Coconut, Guava and Guavaberry. She helps to prepare the fillings for the tarts. Guavaberry – these need to have the seeds removed before stewing. Guavas need to be pealed, split and gutted before stewing.

Coconuts need to have the brown outer skin removed and grated before stewing. Whereas guava berries and guavas need no spices added, coconut need to have cinnamon and vanilla added to the stewing process.

Marie also learns how to make Boyja. This is a heavier type of cake made with cornmeal and ripe bananas.

Figure 11 Brick Oven

Brick Oven

One month later Marie is allowed to light the brick oven. First she takes the moran broom and sweeps the old ashes out. Then she sets the wood for lighting the oven. The oven will heat from front to back. She sets lighter wood in the back with proper wood fire in the front. She places spray underneath with heavier wood on top. As the fire lights it will heat the front of the oven and the back will also start to heat so that by the time the fire reaches the back the whole oven should be well heated. Marie learns that the front will cool faster than the back and that is why we need it to be the hottest area in the beginning. When the bricks at the top of the oven turn white it is ready.

You need to sweep out all the fire from the oven. Do not clear the ash pit as this will help the oven to hold heat longer.

Figure 12 Moran broom

Marie takes the Moran broom and sweeps the fire and ashes from the oven, then Miss Wilda shows her how to use the peal to add the items to be baked.

Figure 13 Placing items in the brick oven to bake

When all the items are in the oven the door is shut, soon the mouth watering smells of items baking fill the air. Marie feels so proud she is baking it smells just like when she is at home and Miss Wilda baking. Marie can't keep the smile from her face.

Over the next couple of years Marie continues to learn all she can from Miss Wilda. Soon she has developed a style of her own, and some of Miss Wilda's customers have started to order items made by her. Her Boyja is one item that has customers coming back each week for more.

One day when she arrives to assist with the baking, Miss Wilda says to her, I notice you have a nice young man courting you. Soon you will be getting married. Marie blushes and answers 'Not for a couple of years. He will need to finish building his house.'

'There is nothing more that I can teach you.' says Miss Wilda. You even have customers of your own; it is time for you to start operating as an independent baker. So, you can have a nest egg for when you get married. You can use my oven until you can have one built for yourself.

'My young man is building one for me by the house where we are going to live.' Marie said, blushing even harder.

'You were a good pupil and I am proud to have been the one who thought you to bake.'

A big smile breaks out all over Marie's face and she begins to hop and dance around as she shouts 'I am a baker, a baker, a baker. I am a baker, a baker, a baker. Thank you, Miss Wilda, for helping me to achieve my dream. I am a baker, a baker, a baker.' She continues to sing as she pumps her fist in the air.

'Yea-a-a-a-a-a-h, I am a baker.'

Marie got married at age eighteen. Her wedding was a big celebration that lasted a week with much eating and drinking. When she moved into the new home that her husband had built, she was so happy. She had a nice two room house with a separate kitchen. There she was able to continue to bake all the lovely items she had learned from Miss Wilda. As one of the best bakers in the village she was able to teach other young ladies her craft and had what the villagers called Marie's Bakery and

Baking School. Young ladies even came from other islands to learn from her.

One day as Marie took a break to wipe the sweat from her dripping brow, she paused and reflected on how far she had come. She admired the bustle in her yard as young ladies prepared the items to be placed in the oven. She smiled and thought to herself. I am truly a baker. She whispers, 'thank you God for fulfilling my dream.'

Marie's Recipes

Sweet Potato Pudding

3 lb Sweet Potato

¼ lb Pumpkin

1 Dry Coconut grated (set aside I cup to be added to pudding. Pour hot water over the rest to make coconut milk)

1 cup coconut milk

1 small tannia (optional)

I large green Banana (optional)

¼ cup flour

Salt (to taste)

Sugar (sweeten to taste)

2 oz lard and butter (melted)

Black Pepper (to taste)

Sugar and water mixture

Method

Peel, wash and grate potatoes, pumpkin, tannia, and banana together. Add grated coconut and stir well, squeeze coconut and strain to gather milk, add slowly to mixture until it looks like a thick soup. Add salt and sugar to taste. Add Black pepper to taste. Pour into a greased baking pan and bake in back of oven until a knife inserted in the center comes out clean. Remove from oven and pour a mixture of sugar and water over pudding leave to cool.

Coconut Bread

3 cups grated Coconut

1 tsp salt

¾ cup sugar

4 cups flour

½ shortening (Butter and Lard)

3 tsp baking powder

Method

Sift flour and baking powder together. Add coconut, sugar and shortening, Mix water and salt to taste. Add enough water to make a stiff dough. Knead on floured board until smooth. Divide dough into two equal halves and make into two round balls. Lightly flour surface. Lightly flour rolling pin and roll each ball until they are 1 inch thick. Using a fork or a knife make a number of small holes in the surface of each bread. Place bread in a greased baking tin and place in front of oven and bake until brown. Baked bread should make a hollow sound when tapped.

This recipe can be used to make Gini corn and cornmeal breads. It can be made plain without only flour for a powder bread.

Boyja

4 Ripe bananas mashed

1 lb. Cornmeal

2 tbs Baking Powder

1lb Flour

½ cup Lard {melted}

½ Butter (melted)

1 grated coconut (set aside 1 cup for adding to bouja, add rest to water to make coconut milk)

4 cups Water

Salt to taste

Sugar to taste

Method

Mix flour, cornmeal, and baking powder together. Add coconut milk and mix well. Add bananas, melted lard and butter and coconut. Season to taste with salt and sugar. Pour mixture into a greased and floured pudding pan. Bake in back of oven until a knife inserted in the center comes out clean.

Tart

3 cups flour

¼ cup butter

½ cup brown sugar

Pinch of salt

2 tsp baking powder

1 tsp Vanilla essence

1 tsp cinnamon

1 egg (optional)

Milk

Method

Beat sugar and butter together until sugar melts. Add egg, salt, baking powder, and cinnamon, mix well, add flour and enough milk to make a stiff dough. Do not knead, pound and mix until smooth. Lightly flour board and rolling pin. Roll dough until about ½ inch thick. Roll one end of dough around rolling pin and fit into greased and floured tart plate. Trim excess dough from around edges and fill center with filling (pineapple, guava, coconut, guava berries) decorate top with thin strips of dough. Cut and place a strip around the edge of the tart plate. Use a wet knife or fork to lightly press it in place. Bake in front of oven until lightly browned.

Pound cake

1lb flour

1lb butter

1lb sugar

6 eggs

2 tbs vanilla

1 tea spoon brandy or peel of one lime

1 cup milk

Method

Cream butter and sugar together until light (this will ensure that the sugar melts and is not still individual grains). Beat eggs until light and add brandy or lime peel to eggs (this will cover the natural smell and flavour of the eggs). Add eggs to butter and sugar mixture a little at a time. Add flour at the same time. Add Vanilla and milk and mix until smooth. Grease and flour pudding pan and pour mixture into pan. Bake in back of oven until a knife inserted in the center comes out clean.

Yeast Bread

1 tbs yeast

1 tsp salt or salt water to taste

1 tsp sugar

2 cups warm water

½ cup of lard

5 cups flour

Method

In a calabash or cup place warm water. It must not be too hot or it will kill the yeast. It should not be hotter than you would use to bathe a baby. Add sugar and yeast to water and stir. Set aside to rise.

Place all other ingredients in a dish pan. Mix together. Make a hole in the middle. When yeast rises to the top of the water slowly add to the ingredients in the dish pan, mixing from the middle until all the yeast has been added.

Sprinkle flour on bread board. Place dough on board and begin kneading. If dough sticks to fingers continue adding small amounts of flour until you have a dough that does not stick to your hand. Continue kneading until smooth. Grease pudding pan, make dough into a ball and place in pan. Cover with a cloth.

Leave to rise. When it is about twice its size turn it back out on the board. Using a knife cut pieces in the sizes that you want. Shape breads and place in greased baking pans to rise. When risen they are ready for baking.

www.ingramcontent.com/pod-product-compliance
Lightning Source LLC
Chambersburg PA
CBHW050816090426
42736CB00021B/3469